A New Tune A Day™
for Alto Saxophone

The saxophone edition of *A New Tune A Day* is designed to be used seamlessly with the clarinet edition.

Teachers wishing to accommodate both instruments in a lesson will be able to do so with almost every piece of every lesson, including the duets and rounds, except where indicated: ✳

look for this symbol within the book

The useful addition of chord symbols in the concert key for many of the pieces in this book will enable the teacher to provide an accompaniment on guitar or piano.

Boston Music Company

EXCLUSIVELY DISTRIBUTED BY

HAL•LEONARD®

Foreword

Since its appearance in the early 1930s, C. Paul Herfurth's original *A Tune A Day* series has become the most popular instrumental teaching method of all time. Countless music students have been set on their path by the clear, familiar, proven material, and the logical, sensibly-paced progression through the lessons within the book.

The teacher will find that the new books have been meticulously rewritten by experienced teachers: instrumental techniques and practices have been updated and the musical content has been completely overhauled.

The student will find clearly-presented, uncluttered material, with familiar tunes and a gentle introduction to the theoretical aspects of music. The books are now accompanied by audio CDs of examples and backing tracks to help the student develop a sense of rhythm, intonation and performance at an early stage.

As in the original books, tests are given following every five lessons. Teachers are encouraged to present these as an opportunity to ensure that the student has a good overview of the information studied up to this point.

The following extract from the foreword to the original edition remains as true today as the day it was written:

The value of learning to count aloud from the very beginning cannot be over-estimated. Only in this way can a pupil sense rhythm. Rhythm, one of the most essential elements of music, and usually conspicuous by its absence in amateur ensemble playing, is emphasized throughout.

Eventual success in mastering the instrument depends on regular and careful application to its technical demands. Daily practice should not extend beyond the limits of the player's physical endurance — the aim should be the gradual development of tone control alongside assured finger-work.

Music-making is a lifelong pleasure, and at its heart is a solid understanding of the principles of sound production and music theory. These books are designed to accompany the student on these crucial first steps: the rewards for study and practice are immediate and lasting.

Welcome to the world of music!

Published by
Boston Music Company

This book © Copyright 2006 Boston Music Company.

Unauthorized reproduction of any part of this publication
by any means including photocopying is an infringement of copyright.

Edited by David Harrison
Music processed by Paul Ewers Music Design
Original compositions and arrangements by Ned Bennett
Cover and book designed by Chloë Alexander
Photography by Matthew Ward
Models: Matthew Deacon and Fran Roper
Backing tracks by Guy Dagul
CD performance by Ned Bennett
CD recorded, mixed and mastered by Jonas Persson and John Rose

Contents

Rudiments of music

The staff

Music is written on a grid of five lines called a *staff*.

At the beginning of each staff is placed a special symbol called a *clef* to describe the approximate range of the instrument for which the music is written.

This example shows a *treble clef*, generally used for melody instruments.

The staff is divided into equal sections of time, called *bars* or *measures*, by *barlines*.

Note values

Different symbols are used to show the time value of *notes*, and each *note value* has an equivalent symbol for a rest, representing silence.

The **eighth note**, often used to signify a half beat, is written with a solid head and a stem with a tail. The eighth-note rest is also shown.

The **quarter note**, often used to signify one beat, is written with a solid head and a stem. The quarter-note rest is also shown.

The **half note** is worth two quarter notes. It is written with a hollow head and a stem. The half-note rest is placed on the middle line.

The **whole note** is worth two half notes. It is written with a hollow head. The whole-note rest hangs from the fourth line.

Other note values

Note values can be increased by half by adding a dot after the note head. Here a half note and quarter note are together worth a *dotted* half note.

Grouping eighth notes

Where two or more eighth notes follow each other, they can be joined by a *beam* from stem to stem.

Time signatures

The number of beats in a bar is determined by the *time signature*, a pair of numbers placed after the clef.
The upper number shows how many beats each bar contains, while the lower number indicates what kind of note value
is used to represent a single beat. This lower number is a fraction of a whole note, so that 4 represents quarter notes
and 8 represents eighth notes.

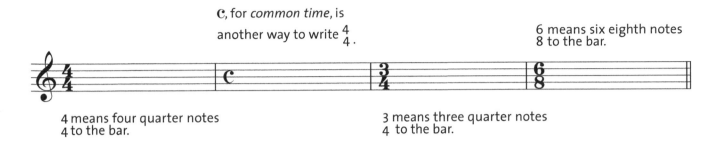

𝄴, for *common time*, is
another way to write 4/4.

6/8 means six eighth notes
to the bar.

4 means four quarter notes
4 to the bar.

3 means three quarter notes
4 to the bar.

Note names

Notes are named after the first seven letters of the alphabet and are written on lines or spaces on the staff,
according to pitch.

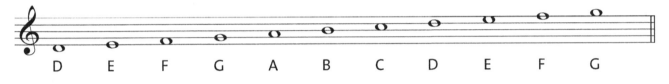

D   E   F   G   A   B   C   D   E   F   G

Accidentals

The pitch of a note can be altered up or down a half step (or *semitone*) by the use of sharp and flat symbols.
These temporary pitch changes are known as *accidentals*.

The *sharp* (♯) raises the pitch of a note.   The *natural* (♮) returns the note to its original pitch.

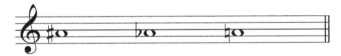

The *flat* (♭) lowers the pitch of a note.

Ledger lines

Ledger lines are used to extend the range of the staff for low or high notes.

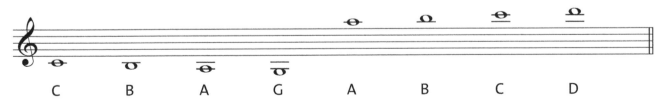

C   B   A   G   A   B   C   D

Barlines

Various different types of barlines are used:

Double barlines divide one section of music from another.   *Final* barlines show the end of a piece of music.

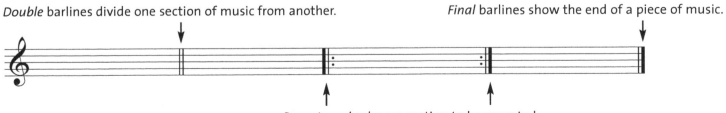

Repeat marks show a section to be repeated.

Before you play:

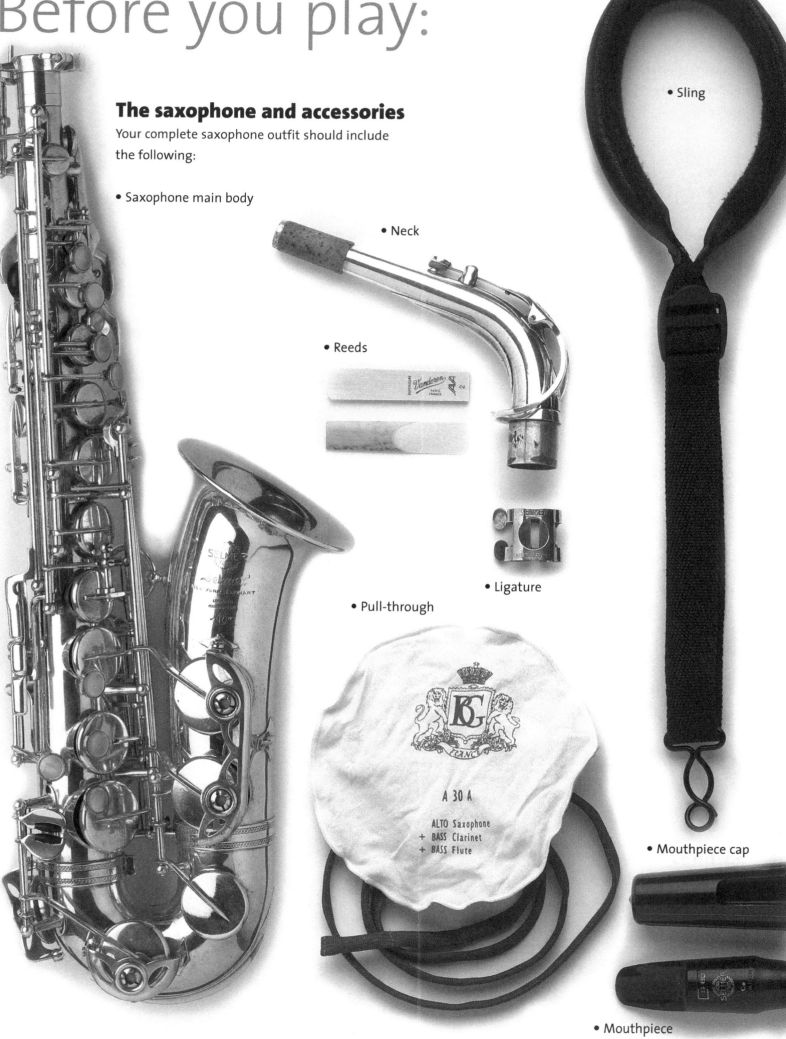

The saxophone and accessories

Your complete saxophone outfit should include
the following:

• Saxophone main body

• Neck

• Reeds

• Sling

• Ligature

• Pull-through

• Mouthpiece cap

• Mouthpiece

Setting-up routine

1. Select a reed that is clean and undamaged (they are quite delicate); place the reed on your tongue, close your mouth and swirl saliva around the reed to moisten it.

2. While you are moistening the reed, push the neck fully into the top of the saxophone so that it extends in line with the thumb hook and rest. Tighten the key so the neck doesn't move. **Never pick the saxophone up by the neck**, just in case the key is not tightened as the body of the saxophone can fall off with disastrous results. Lay the saxophone aside carefully.

3. Attach the reed to the mouthpiece using the ligature. The end of the reed needs to be *exactly* level with and central to the tip of the mouthpiece. This can be a fiddly operation at first.

4. *Twist* the mouthpiece onto the cork at the end of the neck as far as it will comfortably go. Be careful not to dislodge the reed from its position. Make sure the mouthpiece is level when the saxophone is held vertically.

5. Place the sling around your neck, then attach the hook to the ring at the back of the saxophone.

Important *Always* use the pull-through to dry your saxophone after playing.

It's important to make sure that the reed is good and moist before you begin to play.

The ligature should be tight enough to hold the reed firmly. When you've finished playing remove the reed and wipe off excess moisture before replacing it on the mouthpiece.

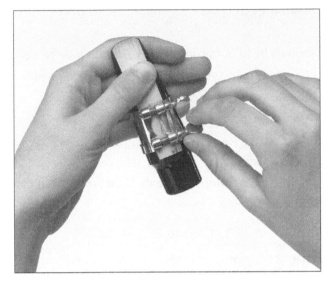

The exact position of the mouthpiece on the neck affects the tuning. Pull the mouthpiece off a little to lower the pitch, and push it on to raise it slightly — don't over-do it.

Spread a little grease on the cork from time to time to prevent cracking.

Lesson 1

goals:

1. **Breathing using the diaphragm**
2. **Posture and hand positioning**
3. **Formation of the mouth shape (embouchure)**

4. **Tonguing**
5. **The notes B, A and G**
6. **Counting while playing; whole notes, half notes, and quarter notes**

Breathing

A relaxed, controlled posture is essential for comfort and correct breathing.

When breathing in and out, always use your diaphragm. This is a large muscular membrane underneath your rib cage which causes your belly to go *out* when breathing in and to go *in* when breathing out.

You will be able to control your breathing far more effectively using your diaphragm than if you were to breathe with the *intercostal* muscles high up in your chest.

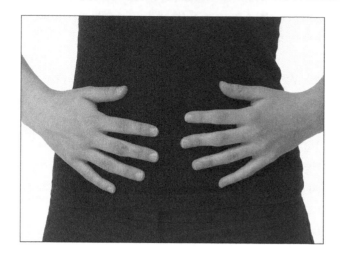

Exercise 1:

Breathe in counting four beats, then breathe out counting 4 and so on, always using the diaphragm and maintaining a steady flow of air.

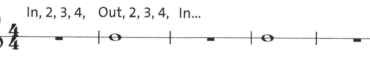

In, 2, 3, 4,   Out, 2, 3, 4,   In...

Place one hand on your stomach to check whether it is going out as you breathe in then in when you breathe out.

Posture and holding the saxophone

Place the saxophone sling around your neck and attach the saxophone to the hook.

Stand in a relaxed, upright way, feet slightly apart.

Place your left thumb on the thumb button towards the top of the saxophone, and your right thumb underneath the curved support towards the bottom.

The fingers of each hand should curl around the body of the saxophone to the front, making sure they do not push against any keys at the sides.

Adjust the sling so that the mouthpiece enters your mouth without you having to crane your neck forwards or back.

Aim to keep a straight back and upright head when playing.

Embouchure

Say the letter *F* as in *foo* several times. Notice how the top teeth push down on the center of the bottom lip.

Rest your top teeth gently on the top of the mouthpiece, about a centimeter or ³⁄₈" from the tip.

Push your bottom lip upwards against the reed without using your bottom teeth as support.

Now close the sides of your mouth around the mouthpiece.

The lips should form a firm, airtight seal around the mouthpiece. Make sure the cheeks remain taught: don't puff them out.

Exercise 2:

Set your top teeth and bottom lip on the mouthpiece. Breathe in through the corners of your mouth over the count of 4, close the mouth and breathe out attempting to produce a note. Don't puff out your cheeks.

- If you are able to play a note, well done – you are on your way!
- If you just hear the sound of air blowing down the saxophone, tighten your embouchure around the mouthpiece a bit, but don't bite.
- If the airway is blocked when you try to play, this is because you are closing the gap between the reed and the mouthpiece. Loosen your embouchure a bit.
- If you make a nasty squeak, it is probably because your bottom teeth are touching the reed. Remember it is the bottom lip that must support the reed.

Tonguing

Say the word *too* several times. The tongue acts as a valve that blocks the air until the precise moment that the word is started. Notes on the saxophone should be started in this way to ensure a clean *attack*.

Breathe in and form the correct embouchure as described above. Place your tongue along the underside of the reed so there is about a centimeter or ³⁄₈" of contact, from the tip of the tongue to the tip of the reed.

Start a note by releasing the tongue from the reed as in the word *too*.
The note should have a definite and tidy beginning.

Exercise 3:

Play the following notes in time, ensuring you tongue each one.

Lesson 1

The notes B, A and G

Take a deep breath and then play the note, holding it for a few seconds.

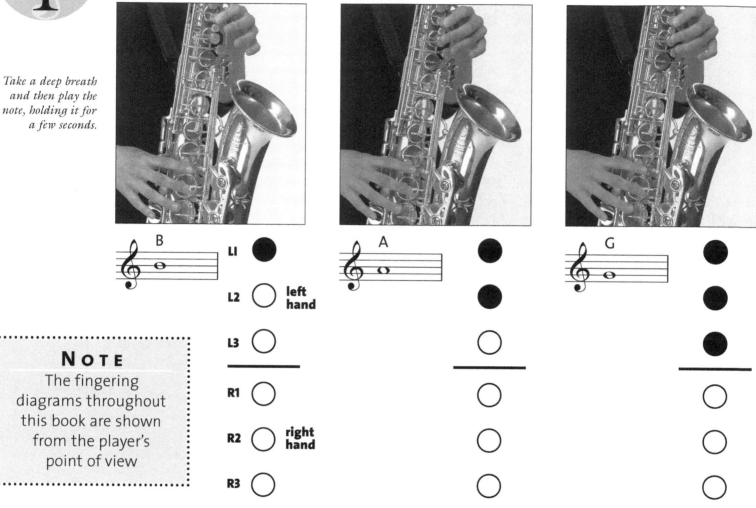

> **N O T E**
> The fingering diagrams throughout this book are shown from the player's point of view

Exercise 4:

Breathe before the beginning of this exercise and in the rests.

Don't forget to tongue each note. A four-beat note is called a **whole note**.

Exercise 5:

Each of the notes and rests here are **half notes,** worth two beats.

Exercise 6:

These notes and rests are all **quarter notes,** worth one beat each.

Breathe in quickly during quarter-note rests.

Pieces for Lesson 1

Valley Song

3

Going Cuckoo

4

Au Clair de la Lune

5-6

goals:

1. **The note C**
2. **Open-throat breathing**
3. **Dotted half notes**
4. **Three beats in a bar**

The note C

> ### OPENING YOUR THROAT
>
> Blow on the back of your hand. You will feel the air is cold. Now try again, pretending that you are steaming up a window. This time the air on the back of your hand should feel warm because you have just breathed out with your throat open. You should keep your throat open at all times when playing as it will improve your tone.

Exercise 1:

Stand with a relaxed posture, take a good deep breath and play the note with an open throat, using the diaphragm to control the air flow.

The symbol above this note is called a **pause**. It means you should hold the note for longer than its actual value of four beats. Hold this one for as long as you can. Play with an **open throat**.

Long notes like this one should be the first thing you practice every day.

Exercise 2:

Play these notes in tempo with an open throat. The little commas are *breath* marks.
Take a very quick breath here without disrupting the 4-beat count.

Exercise 3:

Changing fingers smoothly from C to B and back is very difficult. Play this exercise many times, starting slowly, then playing it more quickly as your coordination improves. Don't be satisfied with any untidiness!

Dotted notes

A dot placed to the right of a note multiplies its duration (value) by one and a half.

This means that a half note with a dot would increase in duration from two beats to three (2+1=3).

Count: 1   2   3   4   1   2   3   4

Exercise 4:

Count carefully as you play these notes. Remember the open throat.

Time signatures

So far all the exercises and pieces have had a **time signature** of four beats to every bar:

1, 2 , 3 , 4 , **1** , 2 , 3 , 4 , **1** , 2 , 3 , 4 etc.

Many pieces, however, contain three beats per bar.

This means that the count in your head will be **1**, 2 , 3 , **1** , 2 , 3 , **1** , 2 , 3 etc.

A waltz is a dance that uses this time signature.

Exercise 5:

Count three beats per bar, as shown by the top number of the time signature, and make sure you don't get confused between notes in spaces (A and C) and notes on lines (G and B).

Count: 1   2   3   1   2   3   1   2   3

> ### THINK!
> Are you still relaxed when you play?
> Remember to keep your shoulders
> down and breathe using your
> diaphragm.
>
> Check that your bottom lip
> is not being drawn inwards when
> you play: the support for the reed
> needs to be in the lip,
> not the bottom teeth.

Check the lip: the support for the reed needs to be in the lip, not the bottom teeth.

Pieces for Lesson 2

7-8 *Back To Bed*

9 *Grumpy Graham*

10 *Medieval Dance*

11 *Barcarolle*

Offenbach

goals:

1. The octave key
2. The note D with the octave key
3. Tied notes

The octave key

You will probably have noticed the only key on the back of the saxophone. This is the octave key and is operated by your left thumb. The thumb must roll upwards onto this key and not be lifted from the thumb rest. You will need to press this key to play all notes above the D that you will learn in this lesson. When you play notes which require the octave key, a little extra air support from the diaphragm will be required, and be careful not to squeeze the reed.

The octave key is used for all notes from this D up. Let the thumb sit on the thumb rest in such a way that you can comfortably press the key down when needed.

The note D

You need three fingers in each hand for this note, as well as the octave key.

Remember to stand comfortably with relaxed shoulders. The modern saxophone is designed so that you shouldn't have to stretch to reach the keys, however make sure you are not pushing any of the keys at the sides of the instrument.

Breathe with the diaphragm and with an open throat. Increase the support in your bottom lip a little.

Exercise 1:

Play this one a few times, holding the note for as long as is comfortable.

Exercise 2:

Remember to tongue the beginning of each note.

15

Exercise 3:

Play this one many times to ensure that your tongue, fingers and thumb (if needed) all move together.

Exercise 4:

Don't get confused between G, B and D, which all look a bit similar.

Ties and tied notes

Two notes of the same pitch can be joined together to make a longer note by *tying* them together. A curved line is drawn from one to the other to show this. The note is then held on for the *combined value* of the two notes. This is usually needed if a note needs to carry on into the next bar.

Here are some examples:

is held for **3** beats   is held for **6** beats

Exercise 5:

Count very carefully here.

Count: **1   2   3   4   1   2...**

THINK!

Are you playing with *warm air* because your throat is open?

Is your thumb rolling to push the octave key, not lifting?

Pieces for Lesson 3

Jingle Bells

12–13

Largo (from the *New World Symphony*)

Dvořák

14–15

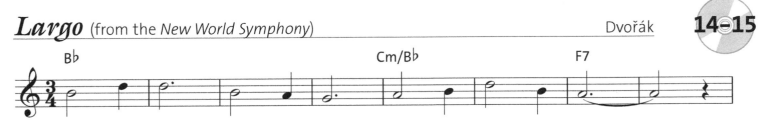

Lightly Row

16

Student / Teacher

Knight Time

17–18

Lesson 4

goals:

1. The note E with the octave key
2. Dynamics (loud and soft)
3. Slurred notes

The note E

E

Remember to roll your thumb to the octave key, and to use your diaphragm to provide a little extra air for these higher notes.

Exercise 1:

Rolling the octave key.

Dynamics

Notes and rhythms are two of the elements of music, but without expression, music can be lifeless and mechanical. One of the obvious ways of introducing *color* into music is to play sections of pieces or phrases at different levels of loudness.

f stands for the word *forte* and means loud.

p stands for the word *piano* which means quiet.

Exercise 2:

Play these notes according to the dynamic displayed underneath.

Use your diaphragm to increase the air flow for the loud notes, and decrease the air flow for the quiet ones.

It's often harder to play a piece slowly and accurately than to bluff your way through it quickly.

Take your time and aim for a clear, confident style.

Exercise 3:

This is a note-twister. Try it slowly at first, then try to build up speed each time you practice it.

Can you play it in one breath?

Exercise 4:

These notes are all written on spaces. Don't get A, C and E confused.

Slurs

In all the pieces and exercises so far you have tongued every note; that is, you have started each note with a *T* as in *too*. This can make the music sound a bit disjointed, and spoils the flow of gentle pieces such as *Barcarolle* in lesson 2.

Music is made smoother by slurring notes together. This means you should only tongue the note where the slur begins. All other notes included in the slur are played by just changing the fingering.
Slurs are shown by lines which look like ties, but the notes will be of different pitches.

Be sure to give a clean, crisp end to your notes by bringing your tongue back onto the reed rather than by just stopping breathing, especially at the end of a piece or at a rest.

Exercise 5: slurred pairs

Only tongue the first of each pair of notes, but keep the air flowing as you play the second.

Exercise 6:

Here you need to slur three notes at a time. The steady 1, 2, 3 count is unaffected by slurs.

Exercise 7:

Try *Barcarolle* again with slurs and with the dynamic shown. It should sound much more like a lullaby.

Pieces for Lesson 4

19-20 ## *When The Saints Go Marching In*

21-22 ## *Joshua Fought The Battle Of Jericho*

Spiritual

23-24 ## *Coventry Carol* (adapted)

Canon For Two

The second player begins one bar behind the first player.

goals:

1. **The note C sharp (C♯)**
2. **Tones and Semitones**
3. **Repeat signs**

The note C♯

As no fingers are required for this note, extra care must be taken to keep the saxophone from moving around. Keep your fingers curled over the front keys, but don't close any of them.

Compare this note with C and D.
You will hear that C♯ is halfway between.

The difference in pitch between C and D is called a **tone**.
C to C♯ is only a **semitone**.
C♯ to D is also a **semitone**.

A semitone is the smallest *interval* that can be played on most instruments.

Exercise 1:

Get used to holding the saxophone when playing C♯.

Exercise 2:

Compare C to D (a tone) with C to C♯ (a semitone). The *natural* sign is to remind you when to play a normal C.

The thick barlines with two dots tell you to **repeat** the music between them—in other words, play twice.

Repeat sign

Exercise 3: sharps and naturals

All the Cs here are natural unless they have a sharp symbol immediately before them or they come after a C♯ in the same bar and don't have a natural sign.

Pieces for Lesson 5

25-26 *Jingle Bells*

27 *Abide With Me*

Monk

Student

Teacher

28-29 *Juggling*

test: *for* Lessons 1 to 5

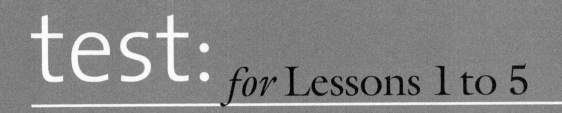

1. Note duration

On the staff below, draw notes of the indicated duration:

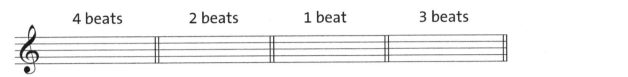

4 beats   2 beats   1 beat   3 beats

(4)

2. Rests

On the staff below, draw rests of the indicated duration:

4 beats   2 beats   1 beat   3 beats

(4)

3. Notes

On the staff below, draw the following notes as half notes:

G, B, E, C, A, D and **C♯**

(8)

4. Sharp thinking

How many **C♯**s do you play in this piece? _____

(2)

5. Bars

Draw barlines on this staff where they are needed.

(7)

Total (25)

goals:

1. **The note F sharp (F♯)**
2. **Key signatures and their meaning**
3. **The keys of C, G and D majors**

The note F♯

This note is a semitone below G.

Exercise 1:

Listen to how close F♯ and G sound.

Exercise 2: wide leaps

Although the notes are a long way from each other, only a few fingers have to move. Play this as cleanly as you can.

F♯

Different keys

If you try to sing a simple tune such as *The Star Spangled Banner*, you may find early on that you can't reach the high notes without really straining. The solution is to start the piece a little lower. This time, you may be able to sing the high notes perfectly. You are now singing the piece in a different key.

There are many different keys in music, each of which needs its own set of notes. The key of **C major** is easy as it requires no sharps. The key of **G major** requires all **F**s to be played as **F♯**. The key of **D** requires all **F**s and **C**s to be played as **F♯** and **C♯**. These necessary alterations will be shown as the **key signature** at the beginning of every line of music.

C major

G major

D major

Exercise 3: comparison

Play the opening to this well-known carol first in the key of C major, then in the key of D major.
Notice that the key signature tells you that all Cs are in fact C♯s, otherwise the tune will sound wrong.

C major

D major

Pieces for Lesson 6

Barcarolle

(Learn the bottom part this time!)

Offenbach

11

In Paris

30-31

> ### THINK!
>
> Do you start every practice session with long notes? They are the best way to improve your tone and build up your strength.

Pieces for Lesson 6

When The Saints Go Marching In

The key of this piece is A major, but don't worry about the G♯ in the key signature...
you won't need to play a G♯.

Steal Away

Spiritual

From *The Unfinished Symphony*

Schubert

Count up to 6 in each bar for this one, and watch out for the C♯s!

Pieces for Lesson 6

Nkosi Sikelel'

E. Mankayi Sontonga

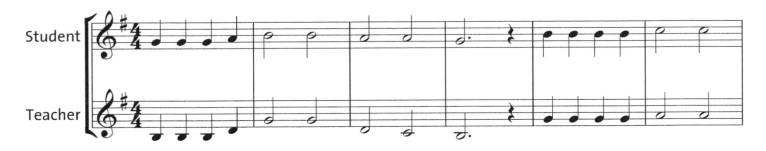

Magnetic Forks

The notes E and D

E

D

Octaves

Practice makes perfect. Perseverance will be rewarded with a good, strong tone.

Make sure you are breathing from your diaphragm for complete breath control, and experiment with your embouchure. And most important of all: relax!

You have already seen how to play the notes D and E in lessons 3 and 4. However, the new notes for this lesson are played without the octave key: they sound the same but rather lower.

Exercise 1:

Compare the sounds of low E with the *higher* E and low D with the *higher* D.

The large $\mathbf{C}$ at the beginning of this staff is shorthand for **common time,** which is the same as $\frac{4}{4}$.

Exercise 2:

Low notes can be hard to play. Ensure that your throat is open. Imagine trying to steam up the inside of the saxophone with your breath.

Pieces for Lesson 7

O Come All Ye Faithful

Skye Boat Song

Scottish traditional

Repeat the section within the repeat signs, then go back to the beginning and play until
the sign *Fine* (Italian for "end").

Scarborough Fair

English traditional

You could play the top part or the bottom part. If you feel ambitious, learn both!

Student 1

Student 2

Lesson 8

goals:

1. **Eighth notes**
2. **D major scale**
3. **Tempo and character markings**

Eighth notes

Sight-reading (playing music that you haven't seen before) is an important skill for a musician.

Get into the habit of finding music you haven't played before and trying to play it straight off. You'll be surprised how much easier this becomes once you get used to it.

Remember to keep a steady beat and the rhythm will take care of itself.

So far you have studied and played notes that last for four beats (whole note), two beats (half note), and one beat (quarter note). You have also learned how to increase note durations by tying notes together or by adding a dot to a half note (for a three-beat note).

Eighth note are notes which last for *half* the length of a quarter note and should therefore be played *twice* as fast.

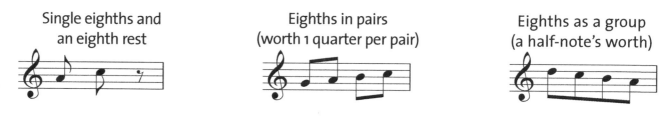

Single eighths and an eighth rest

Eighths in pairs (worth 1 quarter per pair)

Eighths as a group (a half-note's worth)

Exercise 1: *double or quit!*

Keep the beat steady and don't start too quickly.

Count: 1　2　3　4　　1　2　3　4　　1　2　3　4　　1 & 2 & 3 & 4 &　1　2　3　4

Exercise 2: three beats per bar

Count: 1　2　3　　1　2　3　　1 & 2 & 3 &　1　2　3

Exercise 3: the scale of D major

Play your scales steadily and slowly – try to make the notes sound as though they belong together.

A scale is a series of notes that move up or down by step from one note to the same note an octave higher or lower. Play this both slurred and tongued (as shown by the dotted slur lines).

Pieces for Lesson 8

Some short melodies for practice at playing eighth notes.

Yankee Doodle

This piece has only two beats per bar, and notice the tempo (speed) marking above the beginning of the piece.

Can Can

Offenbach

Nessun Dorma

Puccini

From *The Magic Flute*

Mozart

Swing Low, Sweet Chariot

Spiritual

goals:

1. The notes low and high F
2. Dotted quarter notes
3. Anacrusis (upbeat)

The notes low and high F

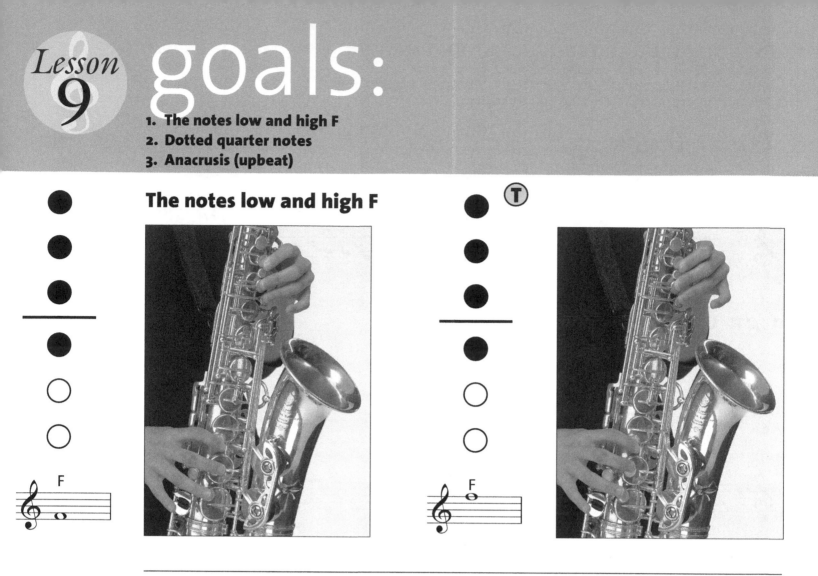

Exercise 1:

Play each note for as long as you can. Every time you practice you should start with long notes!

Dotted quarter notes

Dotted notes are often used instead of tying notes together: the fewer symbols there are on the page, the easier the music is to read.

As long ago as lesson 2 you discovered that a dot placed to the right of a half note increased its value from two beats to three. You could say that the dot *multiplies* its length by one and a half.

The same dot can be used to increase a quarter note's length from one beat to one and a half beats. In other words, instead of being the same length as two eighths tied together, its value is raised to three eighths.

Exercise 2:

Play this slowly so that you can count each eighth note. Learn to recognize the rhythms as you recognize words without really having to read them.

Count: 1   & 2   & 3   & 4   &   1   & 2   & 3   & 4   &   1...

Exercise 3:

Play this exercise a few times increasing the speed a little each time. In time you should feel the rhythm by recognizing the pattern of notes and rely less on having to count each eighth note.

Exercise 4:

Because this type of rhythm is very common but a little tricky, here is another exercise.

This time there are three beats to a bar.

Anacrusis

Sometimes a piece of music doesn't begin with a whole bar.

The next piece begins with a single beat representing the last beat of a bar. This short bar (called an *upbeat* or *anacrusis*) is balanced by another short bar at the end. The two short bars add up to a whole bar.

Pieces for Lesson 9

Auld Lang Syne

Pieces for Lesson 9

Allegro from *Spring* (adapted)

Vivaldi

Allegro is the Italian word for quick and is very commonly seen as a tempo marking in music.

The top line here is the main tune, but you could also learn the bottom line for duet playing.

THINK!
Are you practicing properly?
Always start with long notes, making sure you are using your diaphragm
and open throat. Practice your exercises every day to build up that bottom lip
strength and don't be satisfied if a piece is nearly right.
It needs to be completely right before you should move on.

goals:

1. **The note low C**
2. **More dynamics**

The note low C

As with the other low notes (E and D) you must
ensure that you play this note with an open throat.
It is fun to make this note sound like a fog horn, but
remember that if you can control your breathing
the note will sound just as musical as all the others.

Exercise 1:

Play these long notes with an open throat and
controlled breath.

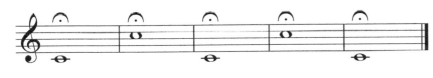

C

Exercise 2:

Here is a *scale* of C major. Practice this first with every note tongued, then with all slurred.
You will need to take a big breath.

More dynamics

Only *p* and *f* have been introduced so far. These tell you to play either quietly or loudly, however, in
between these extremes you could play *moderately quiet* or *moderately loud*.
These are shown by the markings *mp* and *mf*. The *m* is short for *mezzo* which is the Italian word for half.

Exercise 3:

Play these notes with the dynamics indicated.

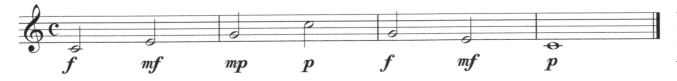

f   *mf*   *mp*   *p*   *f*   *mf*   *p*

*Try to make sure
that the first forte
is exactly as loud as
the second forte:
it's easy to lose track
of just how loud you
are, especially when
the dynamics vary
so much.*

*Watch out that your
mp isn't too quiet,
otherwise you won't
be able to come down
further for the p.*

Pieces for Lesson 10

 58–59 *Silent Night*

Gruber

Watch out for the low C at the end. Don't wake everybody up!

60–61 *Dixie*

Emmett

62 From *Symphony No.9* (play either part)

Beethoven

test: *for* Lessons 6 to 10

1. Note duration

On the staff below, draw notes of the indicated duration:

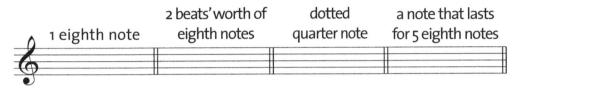

1 eighth note   2 beats' worth of eighth notes   dotted quarter note   a note that lasts for 5 eighth notes

(8)

2. Scale

On the staff below, draw the D major scale including the correct key signature:

(4)

3. Notes

On the staff below draw the following notes as quarter notes:

C, low C, high E, F♯, low D, high F, B, C♯

(4)

4. Dynamics

What are the Italian words for:

Moderately loud _____

Moderately quiet _____

(4)

5. Naming ceremony

Identify all the items indicated by arrows.

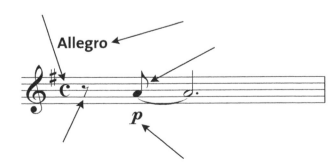

(5)

Total (25)

goals:

1. **The note B flat (B♭)**
2. **The key of F major**

B♭

The note B♭

The **flat** symbol *lowers* the note to which it applies by one semitone. This means that B♭ is a semitone below B, and a semitone above A.

Exercise 1:

Keep covering the keys at the front of your right hand when pushing the side key with the top of your palm.

Exercise 2:

The key signature of F major is one flat: B♭. Practice this scale both tongued and slurred.

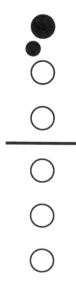

There is an alternative fingering (see left) for the note B♭ that conveniently uses just one finger, which covers the *bis* key as well as the normal B.

This may feel strange at first, but you should get used to it as soon as possible. Try exercises 1 and 2 with this fingering instead.

In general, use the bis key for all B♭s unless there is a B natural (B♮) just before it or just after it.

Exercise 3:

Side B♭ or bis B♭?

B♭

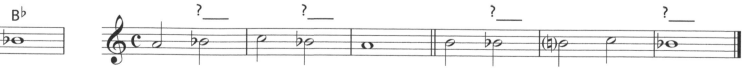

Pieces for Lesson 11

Frère Jacques

French traditional

Up to four people can play this as a round. Begin when the previous instrument reaches the star in the third bar. Use the bis key for B♭ at all times here.

Romance No.1

Beethoven

Both fingerings for B♭ are needed in this piece.

Can Can

Offenbach

Compare this version in F major with the one in D major in lesson 8.

Lesson 12

goals:

1. **The notes G, A, B, and C with the octave key**
2. **The note high D**
3. ***D.S. al Fine***

The notes G, A, B, and C with the octave key

You might find that these high notes sound a little out of tune when you first play them.

Keep a firm embouchure to ensure a steady tone and correct tuning.

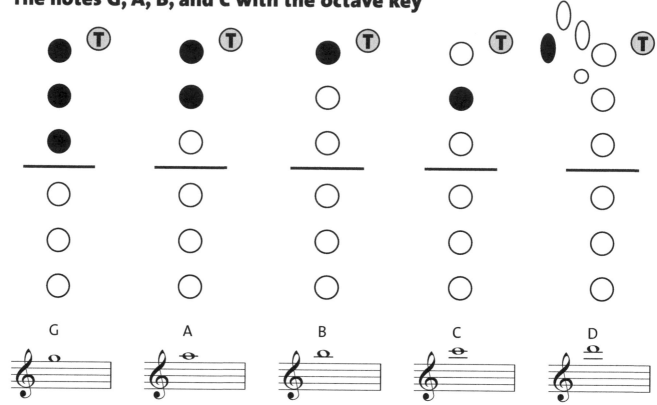

Exercise 1:

There are some wide leaps in this exercise. Remember to keep the tone even.

Exercise 2:

Make sure these octave leaps remain in tune as you go up.

Exercise 3:

Recognizing higher notes.

Pieces for Lesson 12

When The Saints Go Marching In

Play the section between the repeat bars twice. The first time, play the two bars at the end labeled 1, the second time play the bars labeled 2. These are called *first and second time endings*.

Reveille

Military traditional

D.S. al Fine means go back to the sign (𝄋) and play again until *Fine* (end).

goals:

1. **The note F♯ with the octave key**
2. **Finger dexterity**

F♯

The note F♯ with the octave key

Fast fingers

This is the *"don't run before you can walk"* bit.

In order to play fast pieces, you must first spend time playing exercises and pieces slowly in order to gain complete control over every muscle that is being used.

Exercise 1:

This may seem easy, but aim for a perfect tone and precise finger movement.

Exercise 2:

Coordinating your right-hand fingers to play F to F♯ can be hard. Be really critical of yourself: if it's not entirely perfect more practice is needed.

Exercise 3:

Play this many times to build up speed.

Practice will help to build up "muscle memory": eventually you won't have to think about which fingers are required for a particular note, as your hands will "know" what to do.

Exercise 4:

Build up speed until you can play this really quickly.

Exercise 5: scales of G and C major

Every aspect of this must be perfect.

Pieces for Lesson 13

Camptown Races

Foster

68

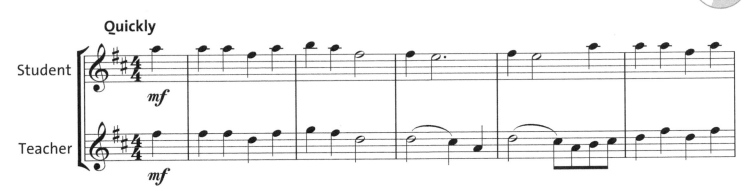

Home On The Range

69–70

Pieces for Lesson 13

71–72

Danny Boy

Irish traditional

This is one of the most beautiful tunes ever written. Spend time on this to ensure complete fluency, control of dynamics and the correct slurs – it will be time well spent.

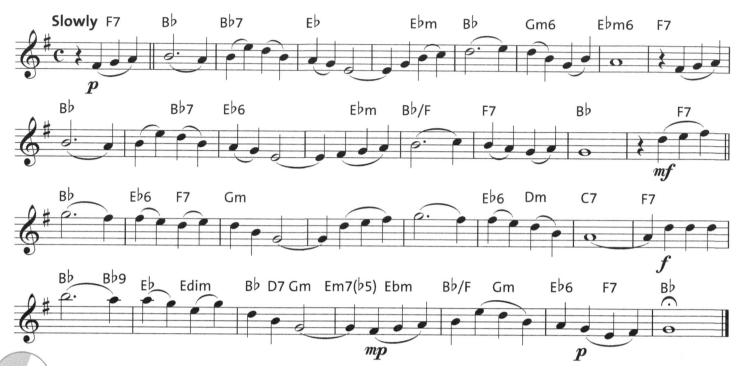

73

Swing Low, Sweet Chariot

Spiritual

goals:

Lesson 14

1. **The note G sharp (G♯)**
2. **Minor keys and scales**

The note G♯

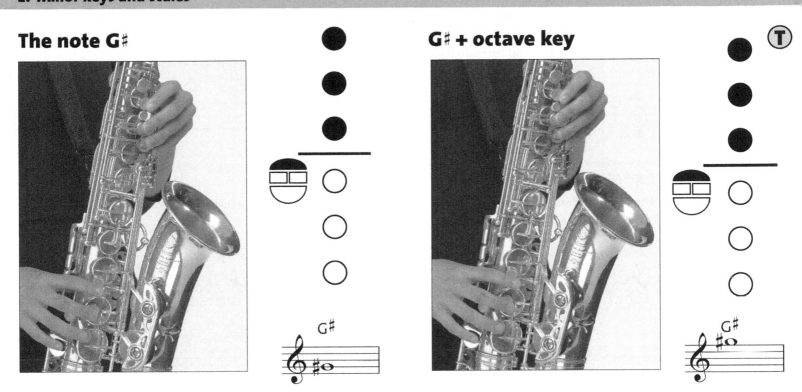

G♯ + octave key

Exercise 1: low G, G♯ and A

This really works your little finger!

Try playing in front of the mirror to keep an eye on which key your left hand little finger should be playing. Eventually the placement of fingers will come naturally.

Exercise 2:

The more you practice the G♯, the stronger your little finger will become, so here goes:

Exercise 3:

The following piece does not appear in the Clarinet book

A finger-twisting Scottish tune.

Major and Minor

Most of the pieces you have played up to now have sounded cheerful. That is because they are virtually all in a *major* key, C major, F major, G major and so on. Sometimes, however, a composer wishes to express sadness in a piece. In general he or she will do this by writing the piece in a *minor* key.

Exercise 4: the A major scale

Play this a few times and listen to its bright character.

Some people think of major keys as being bright, while minor keys are dark.

The mood created has to do with the sequence of intervals that makes up the scale for the key.

Exercise 5: A minor

The *key signature* is the same as C major, however look out for the G♯s which are shown as they occur in the music. (These are called **accidentals**.)

Pieces for Lesson 14

 74-75

Hava Nagila

Israeli traditional

A famous tune in a minor key (Dm). Start slowly and get faster as you go along.
This should sound very exciting!

Pieces for Lesson 14

Go Down Moses

Spiritual

The melody is divided up among the three saxophones so they are all equally important.

Use the written dynamics to blend in when you are playing an accompanying line.

Lesson 15 goals:

1. The notes C♯ and E with the octave key
2. Staccato and legato

The note C♯

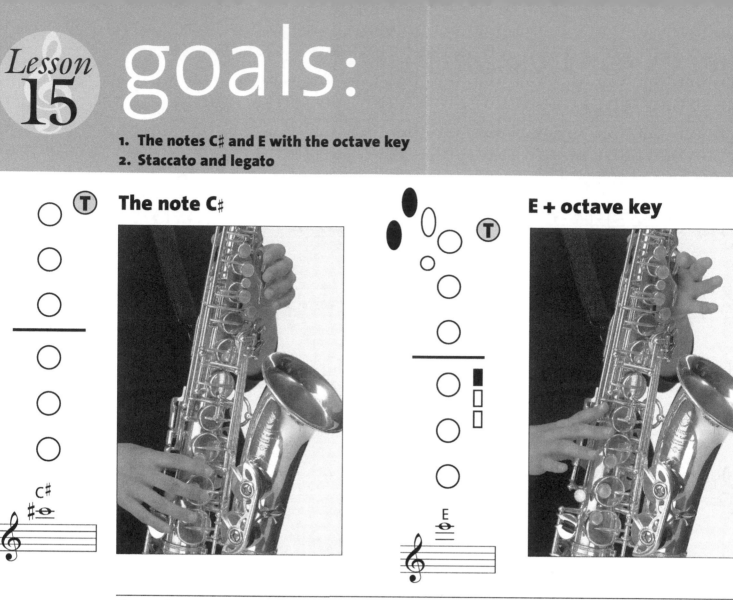

C♯

E + octave key

E

Exercise 1:

High notes only use a very short length of the instrument to make a sound. For this reason they need less breath for the same volume than a low note. Be careful not to use too much breath on high notes, otherwise it may affect the tone and the tuning — and your ears!

Remember diaphragm support for high notes and don't tighten the embouchure.

Keep your fingers close to the sax.

Exercise 2:

This is an E minor arpeggio extending over two octaves.

Exercise 3: low and high

Play slowly to ensure a warm and even tone for all notes.

Staccato and legato

Legato means "joined up" and refers to notes that are slurred or tongued smoothly without a gap from the previous one. *Staccato,* on the other hand, means "detached." This is shown by a dot above or below the note.

Exercise 4:

Repeat this many times to achieve clear staccato tonguing.

Exercise 5:

Begin this very slowly otherwise the eighth notes will be too fast to tongue.

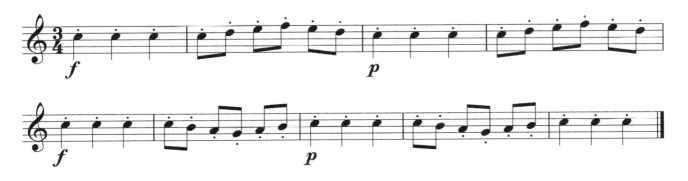

Pieces for Lesson 15

The Blue Danube Waltz
Johann Strauss II

Steadily

Pieces for Lesson 15

78-79 *Oh! Susannah*

Stephen Foster

80-81 *Song Of The Volga Boatmen*

Russian traditional

82-83 *Mango Walk*

Jamaican traditional

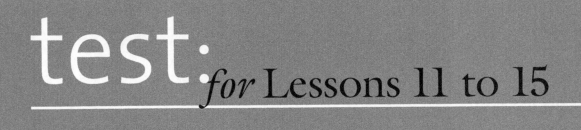

1. Key signatures

On the staff below, draw the correct key signatures for:

G major   F major   A minor   A major   C major

(5)

2. Dots

Simplify the music on the left using dots to get rid of the ties.

(5)

3. Notes

On the staff below draw the following notes as quarter notes:

G♯, low C, high D, B♭, F♯, high E

(6)

4. Articulation

What do the following words mean?

legato _____

staccato _____

(4)

5. Naming ceremony

Identify all the items indicated by arrows.

(5)

Total **(25)**

goals:

1. **The notes E flat (E♭) and B♭ with the octave key**
2. **Enharmonic notes**

The notes E♭ and B♭ with the octave key

Compare the three E♭ notes in different octaves.

Try to keep the tone as similar as possible despite the big difference in pitch. They should all sound as though they are coming from the same instrument.

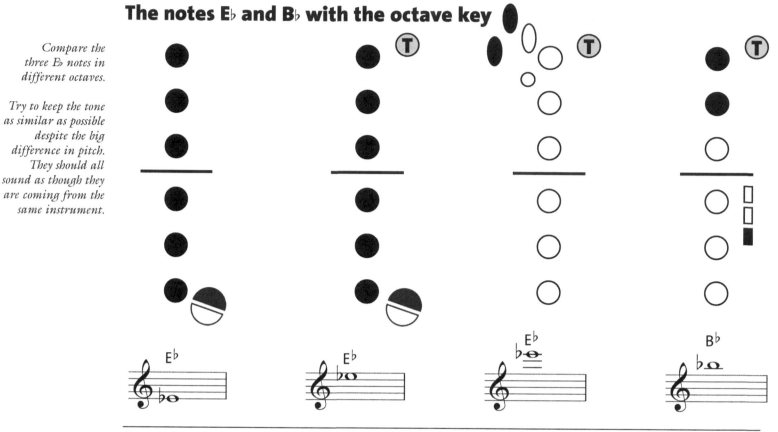

Exercise 1:

Play these long notes. Use a full breath for each one.

Enharmonic notes

From previous lessons, you will know that E♭ is a semitone *below* E, and at the same time a semitone *above* D. This means that the same note could be called D♯. These two notes are *enharmonic equivalents*.

Exercise 2:

These two short pieces need a note you have just learned, the first as a D♯, the second as an E♭.

Exercise 2:

N.B.—Sounds different *in the Clarinet book*

Play the following notes. You *do* know the fingering for each one, however you may need to write down their enharmonic equivalents first.

Gb/_____?   D#/_____?   A#/_____?   Db/_____?

Pieces for Lesson 16

The Entertainer
Scott Joplin

84

Not fast

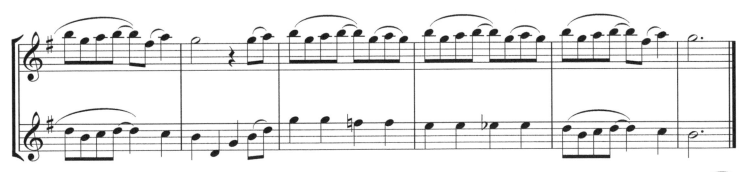

Enharmonic Blues
85-86

Slow blues tempo

1. **Gradation of dynamics**
2. **More Italian terms**

Dynamic markings and tempo markings are very useful.

All dynamic changes you have played so far have been instant. However, suddenly changing from *piano* to *forte* has a different impact from a gradual change.

Music should always be expressive, and these markings will give a clue to the way a piece should be played.

Crescendo means gradually get louder, also shown as: ◁━━━━

Diminuendo means gradually get quieter, also shown as: ━━━━▷

Some other commonly used Italian words to describe a tempo are:

Allegro quickly

Andante at a walking pace

Adagio slowly

Rallentando (rall.) becoming slower

Accelerando (accel.) becoming faster

Pieces for Lesson 17

87 *La Forza del Destino*

Verdi

Andante

Hail The Conquering Hero (from *Judas Maccabeus*)

Handel

Moderato

Fine

D.C. al Fine

William Tell Overture

Rossini

Allegro

D.S. al Fine

1. **Swing eighths**
2. **Playing jazz pieces**

Swing

Remember not to play the eighths too "straight," but instead give them a healthy bounce.

You might imagine the beat divided into three, with the first two-thirds for the first eighth and the final third for the second eighth.

In classical music all eighth notes are played exactly as written, that is, lasting half as long as a quarter note. In jazz, however, eighth notes are normally played unevenly, with the first of each pair longer than half a beat, and the second shorter to compensate. This is called **swing.**

Exercise 1:

Play this E minor scale in swing rhythm. Try it first all tongued, then with the slurs as written.

Pieces for Lesson 18

90–91

Little Brown Jug

92–93

Joshua Jazz

Pieces for Lesson 18

Maryland, My Maryland

94

Moderate swing

Lesson 19

goals:

1. **Good technique through scale practice**
2. **Ensemble playing**

Practicing

Practicing scales every day will help you to:

- Train your fingers to respond quickly in various keys
- Ensure evenness in the timing of notes
- Develop a consistent tone over the instrument's range
- Increase control over your breathing
- Improve your listening awareness of note relationships

The following scales and arpeggios are recommended practice for saxophonists at a relatively early stage. They should be practiced both slurred and tongued.

F major

G major

D major (2 octaves)

D minor

A minor

Pieces for Lesson 19

Gypsy Rover

Pieces for Lesson 19

Down By The Riverside

Lively swing

goals:

1. $^6_8$ time signature (compound time)
2. Traditional-style songs in $^6_8$ time

Simple and compound time

$^2_4$, $^3_4$, and $^4_4$ are all *simple* time signatures.

The top number tells you how many beats per bar, and the bottom number tells you that each beat
is worth one quarter note. This also means that each beat can be divided into **two** eighth notes.

Exercise 1: counting in simple time

Count: 1   2   3   4   1 & 2 & 3 & 4 & 1...

In *compound* time, however, each beat is worth **three** eighth notes.

This means that each beat must now be a *dotted* quarter note.

Exercise 2: counting in compound time

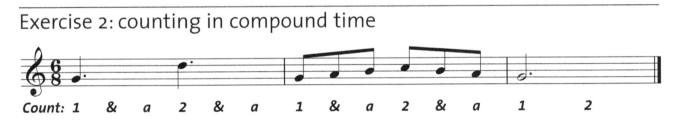

Count: 1   &   a   2   &   a   1   &   a   2   &   a   1   2

Exercise 3:

Here's a well-known tune in $^6_8$ time. Remember to think in *two*.

Count: 1 & a 2 & a   1 & a 2 & a   1 & a 2 & a   1 etc...

Irish jigs are in $^6_8$ time, as is the well-known "We're Off To See The Wizard" from The Wizard Of Oz. $^6_8$ pieces are often lively. Counting two groups of three is much easier than trying to count all six eighth notes.

THINK!

Remember to keep a steady beat.
You might want to use a metronome.
Some people like to tap their foot
when they play, but this takes a little
practice before it comes naturally.

Pieces for Lesson 20

95

The Animals Went In Two By Two

Traditional

Moderato

96–97

For He's A Jolly Good Fellow

Traditional

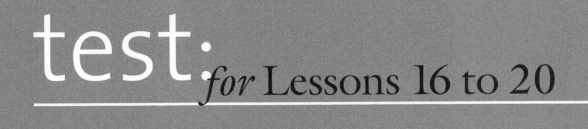

1. Enharmonic

Rewrite the following notes as their enharmonic equivalents:

(5)

2. Afraid of heights?

Write the following music one octave higher:

(6)

3. Breath control

Play this note with a steady tone, controlling your breath at all times.

You will score one point (up to a maximum of five) for every three seconds held.

(5)

4. Expression

Write the Italian words for:

Get louder _____   Get quieter _____

Get quicker _____   Get slower _____

(4)

5. Scale test

Play the following from memory:

1. **D minor scale**

2. **D major arpeggio**

3. **F major scale**

4. **G major arpeggio**

5. **A minor scale**

(5)

Total **(25)**

CD backing tracks

How to use the CD

The tuning note on track 1 is concert A, which sounds the same as F♯ on the alto saxophone. After track 2, which gives an idea of how the alto saxophone can sound, the backing tracks are listed in the order in which they appear in the book. Look for the 💿 symbol in the book for the relevant backing track. Where both parts of a duet are included on the CD, the top part is in one channel, and the bottom part is in the other channel.